CW00594577

BEST OF
THAILAND

Consultant Editor:
Valerie Ferguson

southwater

Contents

Introduction

Thailand is probably one of the most diverse and complex countries in Asia. Geographically it is halfway between India and China and so it is hardly surprising that its national cuisine contains strong influences from these two very different cultures.

A Thai meal offers a combination of contrasting yet complementary flavours: sweet, hot, sour, salty and sometimes bitter. Like native Thais, you should always taste as you prepare in order to achieve the exact balance of flavours that you prefer. Usually, in addition to the obligatory bowl of rice, there will be a variety of dishes including a soup, a curry, a steamed dish, a fried one, a salad and a couple of sauces. All the dishes are placed on the table at the same time and shared.

If you want to serve an authentic Thai meal, there are plenty of fabulous recipes in this book to inspire you. Catering for vegetarian guests is no problem: many of the vegetable and side dishes can be adapted simply by omitting any non-vegetarian ingredients, such as fish sauce, and by adding beancurd (tofu) if you require a more substantial dish.

Try the recipes in this book and share the pride Thais justly feel for their unique and aromatic cuisine.

Ingredients

Many of the ingredients needed to create an authentic Thai meal at home are now widely available in supermarkets; others can be obtained from Asian and specialist shops.

Bamboo Shoots

The edible young shoots of the bamboo plant. When buying canned shoots, look for the whole ones as they seem to be of better quality than the ready-sliced canned shoots.

Banana Leaves

Glossy, dark green leaves of the banana trees are used to line steamers or to wrap foods such as fish before grilling or baking. They impart a slight flavour of fine tea.

Basil

The herb sweet basil is well known in Mediterranean cooking; in Thailand the hotter, slightly medicinal-tasting Thai basil is used frequently.

Beancurd (Tofu)

Made from soya beans, this is sold in blocks packed in water and is available fresh, smoked and dried.

Bean Sauce

Made from salted, fermented soya beans, this sauce is a popular flavouring agent in Asian dishes.

Blachan

A strong-smelling, firm paste made of fermented shrimps, used as a flavouring. To prepare blachan, wrap a piece in foil and dry fry over a gentle heat for 5 minutes, turning occasionally.

Chilli

The small red and green fresh chillies known as Thai or bird's eye chillies are extremely hot. Larger varieties are in fact slightly milder.

Coconut Milk

This unsweetened liquid, made from grated coconut flesh and water, is an essential ingredient of many Thai dishes. It is available in cans, compressed blocks and as a powder.

Coriander

The leaves and seeds of this plant are among the most essential flavourings in Thai cooking. The root is also used.

Fish Sauce

The most commonly used flavouring ingredient in Thai food. It is made from salted anchovies and has a strong, salty flavour.

Galangal

This looks similar to fresh root ginger and is prepared in the same way. It has a wonderful sharp, lemony taste.

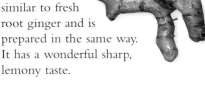

Garlic

Indispensable in Thai cooking. Pickled garlic, available in jars, is also used.

Ginger

Fresh root ginger should be peeled and chopped or crushed before cooking. Though not used as frequently as galangal in Thai cooking, fresh root ginger makes a good alternative.

Kaffir Lime

The fruit is similar to the common lime, but has a knobbly skin. The glossy, dark green leaves impart a pungent lemon-lime flavour to dishes.

Lemon Grass

Similar to a spring onion, this has long, pale green stalks and a bulbous end. It has a woody texture and an aromatic lemon scent. Unless finely chopped, it is always removed from a dish before serving because it is so fibrous.

Tamarind

An acidic tropical fruit that resembles a bean pod, usually sold dried or pulped. To make tamarind juice, soak 25 g/ 1 oz dried tamarind in 150 ml/¼ pint/ ⅔ cup warm water for 10 minutes.

Basic Recipes

These pastes are used continually in Thai cooking. Make up double the quantity and refrigerate for up to 4 weeks, or freeze what is not required.

Red Curry Paste

This paste is used in Thai meat, poultry and vegetable dishes.

Makes about 175 g/6 oz

INGREDIENTS
10 red chillies, seeded and sliced,
    or 7.5 ml/1½ tsp chilli powder
115 g/4 oz dark red onions or shallots, sliced
4 garlic cloves
3 lemon grass stalks, lower part of stem
    sliced and bruised
1 cm/½ in piece galangal, peeled, sliced
    and bruised
4 fresh coriander sprigs, stems only
15–30 ml/1–2 tbsp groundnut oil
5 ml/1 tsp grated dried citrus peel
1 cm/½ in cube blachan, prepared
15 ml/1 tbsp coriander seeds
10 ml/2 tsp cumin seeds
5 ml/1 tsp salt

1 Pound the chillies or chilli powder, onions or shallots, garlic, lemon grass, galangal and the stems from the coriander sprigs in a mortar to a paste, gradually adding the oil. Add the dried citrus peel and blachan.

2 Dry fry the coriander and cumin seeds, then turn them into a clean mortar and grind them to a powder. Add the ground spices to the paste with the salt and mix well.

Green Curry Paste

Make this using the same ingredients as for red curry paste, but with green chillies in place of the red chillies, white onion instead of a red one, and adding the leaves from the coriander to strengthen the colour.

Preparing Lemon Grass

Use the whole stem and remove it from the dish after cooking, or chop the stem finely.

1 Trim the end of the stem and trim off the top, until you are left with about 10 cm/4 in.

2 Split in half lengthways and finely chop or, if the bulb is particularly fresh, thinly slice. Use as required.

Nam Prik Sauce

The most famous of all Thai sauces, this can be served on its own or stirred into plain cooked rice.

Makes 275 g/10 oz

INGREDIENTS

50 g/2 oz/1 cup dried shrimps, soaked in
    water for 15 minutes and drained
1 cm/½ in cube blachan, prepared
3–4 garlic cloves, crushed
3–4 red chillies, seeded and sliced
50 g/2 oz peeled cooked prawns (optional)
a few sprigs of fresh coriander
8–10 tiny baby aubergines, stalks removed
45–60 ml/3–4 tbsp lemon or lime juice
30 ml/2 tbsp fish sauce, or to taste
15 ml/1 tbsp brown sugar, or to taste

1 Pound the shrimps, blachan, garlic and sliced chillies together in a mortar. Add the fresh cooked prawns, if using, and the coriander. Pound the ingredients again until well combined.

2 Add the aubergines to the mortar and pound into the sauce. Add the lemon or lime juice, fish sauce and sugar to taste, plus a little water if a thinner sauce is required.

Preparing Chillies

Fresh chillies add a distinctive flavour, but remove the seeds before slicing the flesh as they are fiery-hot.

1 Always protect your hands when preparing fresh chillies, as the juice can irritate the skin; wear rubber gloves and be careful never to rub your eyes after handling chillies. Halve the chilli lengthways and remove and discard the cluster of seeds.

2 Slice and finely chop the chilli flesh and use as required. Wash the knife and chopping board thoroughly in plenty of hot, soapy water. Always wash your hands immediately after preparing chillies, even if you have been wearing rubber gloves.

Fish Cakes with Cucumber Relish

These wonderful small fish cakes are a very familiar and popular appetizer. They are usually served with Thai beer.

Makes about 12

INGREDIENTS
300 g/11 oz white fish fillet, such as cod, cut into chunks
30 ml/2 tbsp red curry paste
1 egg
30 ml/2 tbsp fish sauce
5 ml/1 tsp sugar
30 ml/2 tbsp cornflour
3 kaffir lime leaves, shredded
15 ml/1 tbsp chopped fresh coriander
50 g/2 oz green beans, finely sliced
oil, for frying
Chinese mustard cress, to garnish

FOR THE CUCUMBER RELISH
60 ml/4 tbsp Thai coconut or rice vinegar
60 ml/4 tbsp water
50 g/2 oz sugar
1 pickled garlic head
1 cucumber, quartered and sliced
4 shallots, finely sliced
15 ml/1 tbsp finely chopped fresh root ginger

1 To make the cucumber relish, bring the vinegar, water and sugar to the boil. Stir until the sugar dissolves, then remove from the heat and cool.

2 Combine the rest of the relish ingredients in a bowl and pour over the vinegar mixture.

3 Put the fish, curry paste and egg in a food processor and process well. Transfer the mixture to a bowl, add the rest of the ingredients, except the oil and garnish, and mix well.

4 Mould and shape the mixture into cakes about 5 cm/2 in in diameter and 5 mm/¼ in thick.

5 Heat the oil in a wok or deep-fat fryer. Fry the fish cakes for 4–5 minutes. Remove and drain. Garnish with Chinese mustard cress and serve with the cucumber relish.

Steamed Seafood Packets

Very neat and delicate, these little steamed packets make an excellent starter or a light and unusual lunch dish.

Serves 4

INGREDIENTS
225 g/8 oz crab meat
50 g/2 oz shelled prawns, chopped
6 water chestnuts, chopped
30 ml/2 tbsp chopped bamboo shoots
15 ml/1 tbsp chopped spring onion
5 ml/1 tsp chopped fresh root ginger
15 ml/1 tbsp soy sauce
15 ml/1 tbsp fish sauce
12 rice sheets
banana leaves, or foil
oil, for brushing
2 spring onions, shredded, 2 red chillies, seeded and sliced, and fresh coriander leaves, to garnish

1 Combine the crab meat, chopped prawns, chestnuts, bamboo shoots, spring onion and ginger in a bowl. Mix well, then add the soy sauce and fish sauce. Stir to blend.

2 Take a single rice sheet and dip it in warm water. Place it on a clean flat surface and leave it for a few seconds to soften.

COOK'S TIP: The seafood packets will spread out when steamed, so be sure to space them well apart to prevent them sticking together.

3 Place a spoonful of the seafood mixture in the centre of the sheet and fold into a square packet. Repeat with the rest of the rice sheets and seafood mixture.

4 Use banana leaves or foil to line a steamer, then brush with oil. Place the packets, seam-side down, on the leaves or foil and steam over a high heat for 6–8 minutes or until the filling is cooked. Transfer to a plate, garnish with shredded spring onions, sliced chillies and coriander leaves and serve.

Rice Cakes with Spicy Dipping Sauce

Rice cakes are a classic Thai appetizer. They are easy to prepare and make a useful standby since they keep well in an airtight box.

Serves 4–6

INGREDIENTS
175 g/6 oz/1 cup jasmine rice
350 ml/12 fl oz/1½ cups water
oil, for frying and greasing

FOR THE SPICY DIPPING SAUCE
6–8 dried chillies, seeded and soaked in
    warm water for 20 minutes
2.5 ml/½ tsp salt
2 shallots, chopped
2 garlic cloves, chopped
4 coriander roots
10 white peppercorns
250 ml/8 fl oz/1 cup
    coconut milk
5 ml/1 tsp shrimp paste
115 g/4 oz minced pork
115 g/4 oz cherry tomatoes, chopped
15 ml/1 tbsp fish sauce
15 ml/1 tbsp palm sugar or soft dark
    brown sugar
30 ml/2 tbsp tamarind juice
30 ml/2 tbsp coarsely chopped
    roasted peanuts
2 spring onions, finely chopped

1 Drain the chillies and crush in a mortar with the salt. Add the chopped shallots, garlic, coriander roots and peppercorns and pound the mixture into a coarse paste.

2 Boil the coconut milk until it begins to separate. Add the chilli paste. Cook for 2–3 minutes until it is fragrant. Stir in the shrimp paste. Cook for another minute.

3 Add the minced pork, stirring to break up any lumps. Cook for about 5–10 minutes. Add the tomatoes, fish sauce, sugar and tamarind juice. Simmer until the sauce thickens. Stir in the peanuts and spring onions. Remove from the heat and leave to cool.

4 Wash the rice well. Bring to the boil with the water, then cover and leave to simmer for about 15 minutes. Turn out on to a lightly greased tray and press down. Leave overnight in a very low oven until the rice is completely dry and firm.

5 Remove the rice from the tray and break into bite-size pieces. Heat the oil and deep fry the rice cakes in batches for about 1 minute, until they puff up, taking care not to over-brown them. Drain and serve with the dipping sauce.

Spring Rolls

These crunchy spring rolls are as popular in Thai cuisine as they are in Chinese, and have a delicious pork, prawn and garlic filling.

Makes about 24

INGREDIENTS
4–6 dried Chinese mushrooms, soaked
50 g/2 oz bean thread
   noodles, soaked
oil, for frying
2 garlic cloves, chopped
2 red chillies, seeded and chopped
225 g/8 oz minced pork
50 g/2 oz chopped cooked prawns
30 ml/2 tbsp fish sauce
5 ml/1 tsp sugar
1 carrot, finely shredded
50 g/2 oz bamboo shoots, chopped
50 g/2 oz beansprouts
2 spring onions, chopped
15 ml/1 tbsp chopped fresh coriander
30 ml/2 tbsp flour
24 x 15 cm/6 in square spring
   roll wrappers
freshly ground black pepper
spring onions, carrots and red chillies,
   cut in slivers, to garnish
sweet chilli sauce, to serve (optional)

1 Drain and chop the mushrooms. Cut the drained noodles into short lengths, about 5 cm/2 in.

2 Heat 30 ml/2 tbsp oil in a wok or frying pan, add the chopped garlic and chillies and fry for 30 seconds. Add the minced pork, stirring until the meat is browned.

3 Add the noodles, mushrooms and prawns to the wok or frying pan. Season with fish sauce, sugar and freshly ground black pepper. Tip the mixture into a bowl. Mix in the shredded carrot, bamboo shoots, beansprouts, spring onions and chopped fresh coriander until well combined.

4 Mix the flour with a little water to make a paste for sealing the rolls. Place a spoonful of the pork mixture in the centre of a spring roll wrapper. Turn the bottom edge of the wrapper over to cover the filling, then fold in the left and right sides.

5 Roll the wrapper up almost to the top edge. Brush the top edge with flour paste and seal. Repeat with the rest of the spring roll wrappers. Heat some oil and fry the spring rolls a few at a time until crisp and golden brown. Drain. Garnish with slivers of spring onion, carrot and red chilli. Serve with sweet chilli sauce for dipping, if liked.

Spinach & Beancurd Soup

An extremely delicate and mild-flavoured soup that can be a useful choice
of dish with which to counterbalance the heat from a hot Thai curry.

Serves 4–6

INGREDIENTS
30 ml/2 tbsp dried shrimps
1 litre/1¾ pints/4 cups
  chicken stock
225 g/8 oz fresh beancurd (tofu),
  drained and cut into
  2 cm/¾ in cubes
30 ml/2 tbsp fish sauce
350 g/12 oz spinach
freshly ground black pepper
2 spring onions, finely sliced,
  to garnish

1 Rinse and drain the dried shrimps.
Combine the shrimps with the
chicken stock in a large saucepan and
bring the stock to the boil.

COOK'S TIP: This soup is
especially delicious made from
home-made chicken stock. Make up
a large batch and store the rest in
the freezer.

2 Add the beancurd and simmer for
about 5 minutes. Season with fish
sauce and black pepper to taste.

3 Wash the spinach thoroughly in
several changes of water and drain
well. Tear the leaves into bite-size
pieces and add to the soup. Leave the
soup to cook for another 1–2 minutes.

4 Remove from the heat, pour into
soup bowls, sprinkle over the finely
sliced spring onions and serve.

Chicken & Coconut Soup

This soup is rich with coconut milk and aromatic Thai spices.

Serves 4–6

INGREDIENTS
750 ml/1¼ pints/3 cups coconut milk
475 ml/16 fl oz/2 cups chicken stock
4 lemon grass stalks, bruised and chopped
2.5 cm/1 in piece galangal, thinly sliced
10 black peppercorns, crushed
10 kaffir lime leaves, torn
300 g/11 oz boneless chicken, cut into strips
115 g/4 oz/1½ cups button mushrooms
50 g/2 oz baby sweetcorn
60 ml/4 tbsp lime juice
45 ml/3 tbsp fish sauce, or to taste
chopped red chillies, spring onions and fresh
    coriander leaves, to garnish

1 Bring the coconut milk and chicken stock to the boil. Add the lemon grass, galangal, peppercorns and half the kaffir lime leaves, reduce the heat and simmer gently for 10 minutes.

2 Strain the stock into a clean pan. Return to the heat, then add the chicken, mushrooms and sweetcorn. Cook for about 5–7 minutes or until the chicken is cooked.

3 Stir in the lime juice, fish sauce to taste and the rest of the lime leaves. Serve hot, garnished with red chillies, spring onions and coriander.

Hot-&-sour Prawn Soup

Probably the best-known Thai soup, this is flavoured with lemon grass.

Serves 4–6

INGREDIENTS
450 g/1 lb raw king prawns
1 litre/1¾ pints/4 cups chicken stock or water
3 lemon grass stalks, bruised
10 kaffir lime leaves, torn in half
225 g/8 oz can straw mushrooms, drained
45 ml/3 tbsp fish sauce
50 ml/2 fl oz/¼ cup lime juice
30 ml/2 tbsp chopped spring onions
15 ml/1 tbsp fresh coriander leaves
4 red chillies, seeded and chopped

1 Shell and devein the prawns. Rinse the shells, place in a large saucepan with the stock or water and bring to the boil.

2 Add the lemon grass stalks to the stock with half the lime leaves. Simmer for 5–6 minutes until fragrant.

3 Strain the stock, return to the saucepan and reheat. Add the mushrooms and prawns, then cook until the prawns turn pink. Stir in the fish sauce, lime juice, spring onions, coriander, chillies and remaining lime leaves. Serve at once.

Right: Chicken & Coconut Soup (top);
Hot-&-sour Prawn Soup

Sweet-&-sour Fish

The sweet-and-sour sauce, with its colourful tomatoes, complements the strong flavour of the fish beautifully.

Serves 4–6

INGREDIENTS
1 large or 2 medium-size fish, such as
    snapper or mullet, cleaned and
    heads removed
20 ml/4 tsp cornflour
120 ml/4 fl oz/½ cup vegetable oil
15 ml/1 tbsp chopped garlic
15 ml/1 tbsp chopped fresh
    root ginger
30 ml/2 tbsp chopped shallots
225 g/8 oz cherry tomatoes
30 ml/2 tbsp red wine vinegar
30 ml/2 tbsp sugar
30 ml/2 tbsp tomato ketchup
15 ml/1 tbsp fish sauce
45 ml/3 tbsp water
salt and freshly ground black pepper
fresh coriander leaves and shredded spring
    onions, to garnish

2 Heat the oil in a wok or large frying pan and fry the fish for 6–7 minutes on both sides until it is crisp and brown. Transfer to a large serving platter and keep warm.

3 Pour off all but 30 ml/2 tbsp of the oil from the wok or pan and add the chopped garlic, ginger and shallots. Fry until golden, stirring frequently.

4 Add the cherry tomatoes and cook until they burst open. Stir in the red wine vinegar, sugar, tomato ketchup and fish sauce. Simmer the mixture gently for 1–2 minutes and adjust the seasoning according to taste.

1 Score the skin diagonally on both sides of the fish and coat lightly with 15 ml/1 tbsp of the cornflour.

5 Blend the remaining 5 ml/1 tsp cornflour with the water. Stir into the sauce and heat until it thickens, continuing to stir to prevent lumps forming. Pour the sauce over the fish, garnish with coriander and shredded spring onions and serve.

Steamed Fish with Chilli Sauce

Steaming is one of the best methods of cooking fish. Leave the fish whole and on the bone to retain all the flavour and moistness.

Serves 4

INGREDIENTS
1 large or 2 medium firm fish, such as
    bass or grouper, scaled and cleaned
2 banana leaves, or kitchen foil
30 ml/2 tbsp rice wine
3 red chillies, seeded and
    finely sliced
2 garlic cloves, finely chopped
2 cm/¾ in piece fresh root ginger,
    finely shredded
2 lemon grass stalks, bruised and
    finely chopped
2 spring onions, chopped
30 ml/2 tbsp fish sauce
juice of 1 lime

FOR THE CHILLI SAUCE
10 red chillies, seeded and chopped
4 garlic cloves, chopped
60 ml/4 tbsp fish sauce
15 ml/1 tbsp sugar
75 ml/5 tbsp lime juice

1 With a sharp knife, slash the skin of the fish a few times on both sides. Place the fish on a banana leaf or sheet of foil.

2 Mix together all the remaining ingredients and spread over surface of the fish.

3 Put a small, upturned plate in a wok and add 5 cm/2 in boiling water. Place the fish on the leaves or foil in the wok. Cover and steam for 10–15 minutes or until cooked.

4 Place all the chilli sauce ingredients in a food processor and process until smooth. You may need to add a little water if the sauce is too thick.

5 Serve the fish hot, on a banana leaf if liked, with the chilli sauce to spoon over the top.

Baked Fish in Banana Leaves

Fish that is prepared in this way is succulent and flavourful.

Serves 4

INGREDIENTS
250 ml/8 fl oz/1 cup coconut milk
30 ml/2 tbsp red curry paste
45 ml/3 tbsp fish sauce
30 ml/2 tbsp caster sugar
5 kaffir lime leaves, torn
4 x 175 g/6 oz fish fillets, such as snapper
175 g/6 oz mixed vegetables, such as carrots
   or leeks, finely shredded
4 banana leaves or kitchen foil
30 ml/2 tbsp shredded spring onions and
   2 red chillies, finely sliced, to garnish

1 Combine the coconut milk, curry paste, fish sauce, sugar and kaffir lime leaves in a shallow dish. Add the fish fillets and allow to marinate for 15–30 minutes. Preheat the oven to 200°C/400°F/Gas 6.

2 Lay some vegetables on a banana leaf or sheet of kitchen foil. Place a piece of fish on top with a little of its marinade. Wrap up by turning in the sides and ends of the leaf or foil and secure with cocktail sticks. Repeat with the rest of the leaves and fish.

3 Bake for 20–25 minutes or until cooked. Garnish with spring onions and red chillies.

Stir-fried Scallops

Asparagus and scallops are perfect partners in flavour and texture.

Serves 4–6

INGREDIENTS
60 ml/4 tbsp vegetable oil
1 bunch asparagus, cut into 5 cm/
   2 in lengths
4 garlic cloves, finely chopped
2 shallots, finely chopped
450 g/1 lb scallops, cleaned
30 ml/2 tbsp fish sauce
2.5 ml/½ tsp coarsely ground black pepper
120 ml/4 fl oz/½ cup coconut milk
fresh coriander leaves, to garnish

1 Heat half the oil in a wok or large frying pan. Add the asparagus and stir-fry for about 2 minutes. Transfer to a plate and set aside.

2 Add the rest of the oil, the garlic and shallots to the same wok and fry until fragrant. Add the scallops and cook for another 1–2 minutes.

3 Return the asparagus to the wok. Add the fish sauce, black pepper and coconut milk. Stir and cook for another 3–4 minutes or until the scallops and asparagus are cooked. Garnish with coriander and serve.

Right: Baked Fish in Banana Leaves (top); Stir-fried Scallops

Satay Prawns

An enticing and tasty dish. Serve with greens and jasmine rice.

Serves 4–6

INGREDIENTS
450 g/1 lb raw king prawns, shelled, tails left
    intact, and deveined
fresh coriander leaves, 4 red chillies, finely
    sliced, and spring onions, cut diagonally,
    to garnish

FOR THE PEANUT SAUCE
45 ml/3 tbsp vegetable oil
15 ml/1 tbsp chopped garlic
1 small onion, chopped
3–4 red chillies, crushed and chopped
3 kaffir lime leaves, torn
1 lemon grass stalk, bruised
    and chopped
5 ml/1 tsp medium curry paste
250 ml/8 fl oz/1 cup coconut milk
1 cm/½ in cinnamon stick
75 g/3 oz/⅓ cup crunchy peanut butter
45 ml/3 tbsp tamarind juice
30 ml/2 tbsp fish sauce
30 ml/2 tbsp palm sugar or soft dark
    brown sugar
juice of ½ lemon

1 To make the sauce, heat half the oil
in a wok or large frying pan and add
the chopped garlic and onion. Cook
for 3–4 minutes, stirring, until the
onion is soft.

2 Add the chillies, kaffir lime leaves,
lemon grass and curry paste. Cook for
a further 2–3 minutes.

3 Stir in the coconut milk, cinnamon
stick, peanut butter, tamarind juice, fish
sauce, sugar and lemon juice.

4 Reduce the heat and simmer gently
for 15–20 minutes until the sauce
thickens, stirring occasionally.

COOK'S TIP: Commercially made
curry paste has a far superior flavour
to curry powder. Once opened,
it should be kept in the fridge and
used within 2 months.

5 Heat the remaining oil in a separate wok or large frying pan. Add the prawns and stir-fry for 3–4 minutes or until they turn pink and are slightly firm to the touch.

6 Mix the prawns with the prepared sauce. Serve garnished with fresh coriander leaves, sliced red chillies and spring onions.

Stir-fried Prawns with Tamarind

The sour, tangy flavour that is characteristic of many Thai dishes comes from tamarind, a tropical fruit that resembles a bean pod.

Serves 4–6

INGREDIENTS
50 g/2 oz tamarind paste
150 ml/¼ pint/⅔ cup
    boiling water
30 ml/2 tbsp vegetable oil
30 ml/2 tbsp chopped onion
30 ml/2 tbsp palm sugar or soft dark
    brown sugar
30 ml/2 tbsp chicken stock
    or water
15 ml/1 tbsp fish sauce
6 dried red chillies, fried
450 g/1 lb raw shelled prawns
15 ml/1 tbsp fried chopped garlic
30 ml/2 tbsp fried sliced shallots
2 spring onions, chopped,
    to garnish

1 Put the tamarind paste in a small bowl, pour over the boiling water and stir well to break up any lumps. Leave for 30 minutes. Strain, pushing as much of the juice through as possible. Measure 90 ml/6 tbsp of the juice, the amount needed, and store the remainder in the fridge.

2 Heat the oil in a wok or large frying pan. Add the chopped onion and fry until golden brown, stirring occasionally to prevent sticking.

3 Add the sugar, chicken stock or water, fish sauce, fried chillies and the prepared tamarind juice, stirring well until the sugar dissolves. Bring the mixture to the boil.

4 Add the prawns, the fried garlic and shallots. Stir-fry for 3–4 minutes until the prawns are cooked. Garnish with the chopped spring onions and serve immediately.

Stir-fried Chicken with Basil & Chillies

This quick and easy chicken dish is an excellent introduction to Thai cuisine. Deep frying the basil adds another dimension to the dish.

Serves 4–6

INGREDIENTS
45 ml/3 tbsp vegetable oil
4 garlic cloves, sliced
2–4 red chillies, seeded
   and chopped
450 g/1 lb chicken, cut into
   bite-size pieces
30–45 ml/2–3 tbsp fish sauce
10 ml/2 tsp dark soy sauce
5 ml/1 tsp sugar
10–12 fresh Thai basil leaves
2 red chillies, finely sliced,
   to garnish
20 fresh Thai basil leaves,
   deep fried (optional)

2 Add the chicken and stir-fry until it changes colour. Add the fish sauce, dark soy sauce and sugar. Stir-fry for 3–4 minutes or until cooked through.

3 Stir in the fresh Thai basil leaves. Garnish with sliced chillies and the deep fried basil, if using, and serve.

COOK'S TIP: Thai basil leaves take only 30–40 seconds to deep fry.

1 Heat the oil in a wok or large frying pan over a high heat and swirl it around. Add the garlic and chillies and stir-fry for about 30 seconds until golden.

Red Chicken Curry with Bamboo Shoots

Bamboo shoots have a lovely, crunchy texture. It is quite acceptable to use canned bamboo, as fresh bamboo is not readily available in the West.

Serves 4–6

INGREDIENTS
1 litre/1¾ pints/4 cups coconut milk
30 ml/2 tbsp red curry paste
450 g/1 lb diced boneless chicken
30 ml/2 tbsp fish sauce
15 ml/1 tbsp sugar
225 g/8 oz bamboo shoots,
    rinsed and sliced
5 kaffir lime leaves, torn
salt and freshly ground black pepper
2 red chillies, seeded and chopped,
    10–12 fresh basil leaves and
    10–12 fresh mint leaves, to garnish

1 In a large, heavy-based saucepan, bring half the coconut milk to the boil, stirring until it separates.

2 Add 30 ml/2 tbsp of the red curry paste and cook for a few minutes, stirring to blend it with the milk.

3 Add the chicken, fish sauce and sugar. Fry for 3–5 minutes until the chicken changes colour, stirring constantly to prevent it from sticking to the base of the pan.

4 Add the rest of the coconut milk, the bamboo shoots and kaffir lime leaves. Bring back to the boil. Adjust the seasoning to taste. Serve garnished with chopped red chillies and fresh basil and mint leaves.

Sweet-&-sour Pork

Sweet-and-sour is traditionally a Chinese creation, but the Thais do it very well. This version has an altogether fresher and cleaner flavour.

Serves 4

INGREDIENTS
350 g/12 oz lean pork
30 ml/2 tbsp vegetable oil
4 garlic cloves, finely sliced
1 small red onion, sliced
30 ml/2 tbsp fish sauce
15 ml/1 tbsp sugar
1 red pepper, seeded and diced
½ cucumber, seeded and sliced lengthways
2 plum tomatoes, cut into wedges
115 g/4 oz pineapple, cut into small chunks
2 spring onions, cut into short lengths
freshly ground black pepper
fresh coriander leaves and shredded spring
   onions, to garnish

1 Slice the pork into thin strips. Heat the oil in a wok or large frying pan and swirl it around.

2 Add the garlic and fry until golden, then add the pork and stir-fry for 4–5 minutes. Add the onion.

3 Season with the fish sauce, sugar and freshly ground black pepper. Stir to ensure well combined and continue cooking for 3–4 minutes, or until the pork is cooked through.

4 Add the diced red pepper, sliced cucumber, wedges of tomato, pineapple chunks and spring onions. You may need to add a few tablespoons of water if the mixture seems dry. Continue to stir-fry the mixture for another 3–4 minutes. Serve hot garnished with fresh coriander leaves and shredded spring onions.

Special Chow Mein

The *lap cheong* used in this recipe is an air-dried Chinese sausage, available from most Chinese supermarkets. If you find it difficult to obtain, it may be replaced with diced ham, chorizo or salami.

Serves 4–6

INGREDIENTS

45 ml/3 tbsp vegetable oil
2 garlic cloves, sliced
5 ml/1 tsp chopped fresh
    root ginger
2 red chillies, seeded and chopped
2 *lap cheong*, about 75 g/3 oz, rinsed and
    sliced (optional)
1 boneless chicken breast, thinly sliced
16 raw tiger prawns, shelled, tails left
    intact, and deveined
115 g/4 oz green beans
225 g/8 oz beansprouts
50 g/2 oz garlic chives
450 g/1 lb egg noodles, cooked in boiling
    water until tender
30 ml/2 tbsp soy sauce
15 ml/1 tbsp oyster sauce
15 ml/1 tbsp sesame oil
salt and freshly ground black pepper
2 spring onions, shredded, and
    15 ml/1 tbsp fresh coriander leaves,
    to garnish

1 Heat 15 ml/1 tbsp of the oil in a wok or large frying pan and fry the garlic, ginger and chillies. Add the *lap cheong*, if using, and the chicken, prawns and beans. Stir-fry over a high heat for about 2 minutes or until the chicken and prawns are cooked. Transfer to a bowl and set aside.

2 Heat the rest of the oil in the same wok. Add the beansprouts and garlic chives. Stir-fry for 1–2 minutes.

3 Add the egg noodles and toss and stir to mix. Season to taste with soy sauce, oyster sauce, salt and pepper.

4 Return the prawn mixture to the wok. Reheat and mix well with the noodles. Stir in the sesame oil. Serve garnished with spring onions and coriander leaves.

Stir-fried Beef in Oyster Sauce

A simple but delicious recipe, using several types of mushroom.

Serves 4–6

INGREDIENTS
450 g/1 lb rump steak
30 ml/2 tbsp soy sauce
15 ml/1 tbsp cornflour
45 ml/3 tbsp vegetable oil
15 ml/1 tbsp chopped garlic
15 ml/1 tbsp chopped fresh
    root ginger
225 g/8 oz mixed mushrooms, such as
    shiitake, oyster and straw
30 ml/2 tbsp oyster sauce
5 ml/1 tsp sugar
4 spring onions, cut into short lengths
freshly ground black pepper
2 red chillies, seeded and cut into strips,
    to garnish

1 Slice the beef, on the diagonal, into long, thin strips. Mix together the soy sauce and cornflour in a large bowl, stir in the beef and leave to marinate for 1–2 hours.

2 Heat half the oil in a wok or frying pan. Add the garlic and ginger and fry until fragrant. Stir in the beef. Stir to separate the strips, let them colour and cook for 1–2 minutes. Remove from the pan and set aside.

3 Heat the remaining oil in the wok. Add the shiitake, oyster and straw mushrooms. Cook until tender.

4 Return the beef to the wok with the mushrooms. Add the oyster sauce, sugar and freshly ground black pepper to taste. Mix well, then add the spring onions. Serve garnished with strips of red chilli.

COOK'S TIP: Made from extracts of oysters, oyster sauce is velvety smooth and has a savoury/sweet and meaty taste. There are several types available; buy the best you can afford.

Green Beef Curry with Thai Aubergine

This is a very quick curry, so be sure to use good quality meat.

Serves 4–6

INGREDIENTS
15 ml/1 tbsp vegetable oil
45 ml/3 tbsp green curry paste
600 ml/1 pint/2½ cups
    coconut milk
450 g/1 lb beef sirloin, cut into
    long, thin slices
4 kaffir lime leaves, torn
15–30 ml/1–2 tbsp fish sauce
5 ml/1 tsp palm sugar or soft dark
    brown sugar
150 g/5 oz small Thai
    aubergines, halved
a small handful of fresh
    Thai basil
2 green chillies, finely shredded,
    to garnish

2 Gradually stir in half the coconut milk. Cook for about 5–6 minutes, until an oily sheen appears.

3 Add the slices of beef to the saucepan with the kaffir lime leaves, fish sauce, sugar and halved aubergines. Cook for 2–3 minutes, then stir in the remaining coconut milk.

1 Heat the oil in a large saucepan or wok. Add the green curry paste and fry until fragrant, stirring constantly to avoid sticking.

4 Bring back to a simmer and cook until the meat and aubergines are tender. Stir in the Thai basil just before serving, and garnish with green chillies.

Thick Beef Curry in Sweet Peanut Sauce

This curry is deliciously rich and thicker than most other Thai curries. Serve with boiled jasmine rice and salted duck's eggs, if liked.

Serves 4–6

INGREDIENTS
600 ml/1 pint/2½ cups coconut milk
45 ml/3 tbsp red curry paste
45 ml/3 tbsp fish sauce
30 ml/2 tbsp palm sugar or soft dark
 brown sugar
2 lemon grass stalks, bruised
450 g/1 lb rump steak, cut into thin strips
75 g/3 oz/¾ cup roasted ground peanuts
2 red chillies, seeded and sliced
5 kaffir lime leaves, torn
salt and freshly ground black pepper
10–15 fresh Thai basil leaves, to garnish
2 salted duck's eggs, to serve (optional)

3 Continue to cook until the colour deepens. Add the rest of the coconut milk and stir to combine. Bring the mixture back to the boil.

4 Add the strips of beef and the ground peanuts. Stir and leave to cook for 8–10 minutes or until most of the liquid in the pan has evaporated.

5 Add the chillies and kaffir lime leaves. Adjust the seasoning to taste. Garnish with Thai basil leaves and serve with salted eggs, if using.

1 Put half the coconut milk into a heavy-based saucepan and heat, stirring, until it boils and separates.

2 Add the red curry paste and cook until fragrant. Add the fish sauce, sugar and lemon grass.

Water Spinach with Brown Bean Sauce

Water spinach, or Siamese watercress, has arrowhead leaves.

Serves 4–6

INGREDIENTS
1 bunch water spinach, about
    1 kg/2¼ lb in weight
45 ml/3 tbsp vegetable oil
15 ml/1 tbsp chopped garlic
15 ml/1 tbsp brown bean sauce
30 ml/2 tbsp fish sauce
15 ml/1 tbsp sugar
freshly ground black pepper

1 Trim and discard the bottom, coarse, woody end of the water spinach. Cut the remaining part into 5 cm/2 in lengths, keeping the leaves separate from the stems.

2 Heat the oil in a wok or large frying pan. Add the chopped garlic and toss for 10 seconds. Add the stem part of the water spinach, let it sizzle and cook for 1 minute, then add the leafy parts.

3 Add the brown bean sauce, fish sauce, sugar and freshly ground black pepper, and stir well to combine. Toss and turn over the spinach for about 3–4 minutes until it begins to wilt. Serve immediately.

Mixed Vegetables in Coconut Milk

Coconut milk adds richness to the vegetables without masking them.

Serves 4–6

INGREDIENTS
450 g/1 lb mixed vegetables, such as
    aubergines, baby sweetcorn, carrots,
    asparagus and patty pan squash
8 red chillies, seeded
2 lemon grass stalks, chopped
4 kaffir lime leaves, torn
30 ml/2 tbsp vegetable oil
250 ml/8 fl oz/1 cup coconut milk
30 ml/2 tbsp fish sauce
salt
15–20 fresh Thai basil leaves, to garnish

1 Cut the vegetables into similar-size shapes. Put the chillies, lemon grass and kaffir lime leaves in a mortar and grind together. Heat the oil in a wok or large frying pan. Add the chilli mixture and fry for 2–3 minutes.

2 Stir in the coconut milk and bring to the boil. Add the vegetables and cook for about 5 minutes. Season with the fish sauce and salt. Garnish with fresh Thai basil leaves and serve.

Right: Water Spinach with Brown Bean Sauce (top); Mixed Vegetables in Coconut Milk

Beancurd & Green Bean Red Curry

This recipe uses green beans, but you can use almost any kind of vegetable such as aubergines, bamboo shoots or broccoli.

Serves 4–6

INGREDIENTS
600 ml/1 pint/2½ cups coconut milk
15 ml/1 tbsp red curry paste
45 ml/3 tbsp fish sauce
10 ml/2 tsp palm sugar or soft dark
    brown sugar
225 g/8 oz/3 cups button mushrooms
115 g/4 oz/1 cup green beans, trimmed
175 g/6 oz beancurd (tofu), rinsed and cut
    into 4 cm/1½ in cubes
4 kaffir lime leaves, torn
2 red chillies, sliced
fresh coriander leaves, to garnish

1 Cook one-third of the coconut milk in a wok or saucepan until it separates and an oily sheen appears.

2 Add the red curry paste, fish sauce and sugar to the coconut milk. Mix together thoroughly.

3 Add the button mushrooms. Stir and cook for 1 minute. Stir in the rest of the coconut milk and bring the mixture back to the boil.

4 Add the green beans and cubes of beancurd and simmer gently for another 4–5 minutes.

5 Stir in the torn kaffir lime leaves and the sliced red chillies. Serve the curry garnished with the fresh coriander leaves.

Jasmine Rice

This aromatic, long grain rice is the staple of most Thai meals.

Serves 4–6

INGREDIENTS
450 g/1 lb/2 cups jasmine rice
750 ml/1¼ pints/3 cups cold water

1 Rinse the rice thoroughly at least three times in cold water until the water runs clear.

2 Put the rice in a heavy-based saucepan and add the water. Bring to a vigorous boil, uncovered. Stir and reduce the heat to low. Cover and simmer for up to 20 minutes or until all the water has been absorbed. Remove from the heat and leave to stand for 10 minutes.

3 Remove the lid and stir the rice gently with a rice paddle or a pair of wooden chopsticks, to fluff up and separate the grains.

COOK'S TIP: An electric rice cooker cooks the rice and keeps it warm. Different sizes and models of rice cookers are available. The top of the range is a non-stick version, which is a little expensive, but well worth the investment.

Fried Jasmine Rice

The unique pungency of the basil gives this a special Thai flavour.

Serves 4–6

INGREDIENTS
45 ml/3 tbsp vegetable oil
1 egg, beaten
1 onion, chopped
15 ml/1 tbsp chopped garlic
15 ml/1 tbsp shrimp paste
1 kg/2¼ lb/4 cups cooked jasmine rice
350 g/12 oz cooked shelled prawns
50 g/2 oz thawed frozen peas
oyster sauce, to taste
2 spring onions, chopped
15–20 fresh Thai basil leaves, roughly
   snipped, plus an extra sprig, to garnish

1 Heat 15 ml/1 tbsp of the oil in a wok. Add the egg and swirl it around to make a thin pancake. Cook until golden, slide out, roll up and cut into thin strips. Set aside.

2 Heat the remaining oil and fry the onion and garlic for 2–3 minutes. Stir in the shrimp paste. Add the cooked jasmine rice, prawns and peas and stir until heated through.

3 Season with oyster sauce. Add the onions and basil. Serve topped with the pancake strips and a basil sprig.

Right: Jasmine Rice (top); Fried Jasmine Rice

Thai Fried Noodles

Made with rice noodles, this is considered one of the national dishes of Thailand and has a fascinating flavour and texture.

Serves 4–6

INGREDIENTS
45 ml/3 tbsp vegetable oil
15 ml/1 tbsp chopped garlic
16 raw king prawns, shells, tails left intact, and deveined
2 eggs, lightly beaten
15 ml/1 tbsp dried shrimps, rinsed
30 ml/2 tbsp pickled white radish
50 g/2 oz fried beancurd (tofu), cut into small slivers
2.5 ml/½ tsp dried chilli flakes
350 g/12 oz rice noodles, soaked in warm water for 20–30 minutes and drained
115 g/4 oz garlic chives, cut into 5 cm/2 in lengths
225 g/8 oz beansprouts
50 g/2 oz/½ cup roasted peanuts, coarsely ground
5 ml/1 tsp sugar
15 ml/1 tbsp dark soy sauce
30 ml/2 tbsp fish sauce
30 ml/2 tbsp tamarind juice
30 ml/2 tbsp fresh coriander leaves and kaffir lime wedges, to garnish

1 Heat 15 ml/1 tbsp of the oil in a wok or large frying pan. Add the garlic and fry until golden. Stir in the king prawns and cook for 1–2 minutes until pink, tossing from time to time. Remove and set aside.

2 Heat another 15 ml/1 tbsp oil in the wok. Add the eggs and tilt the wok to spread them into a thin sheet. Stir to scramble and break the egg into small pieces. Remove from the wok and set aside with the prawns.

3 Heat the remaining oil in the wok. Add the dried shrimps, pickled radish, beancurd and chilli flakes. Stir briefly. Add the drained noodles and stir-fry for 5 minutes.

4 Add the garlic chives, half the beansprouts and half the roasted peanuts. Season with the sugar, soy sauce, fish sauce and tamarind juice. Mix well and continue to cook until the noodles are heated through.

5 Return the prawn and egg mixture to the wok and mix with the noodles. Serve garnished with the remaining beansprouts and peanuts, coriander leaves and lime wedges.

Crispy Fried Rice Vermicelli

This crisp tangle of fried rice vermicelli, tossed in a piquant garlic, sweet-and-sour sauce, is usually served at celebration meals.

Serves 4–6

INGREDIENTS
oil, for deep frying
175 g/6 oz rice vermicelli
15 ml/1 tbsp chopped garlic
4–6 dried chillies, seeded and chopped
30 ml/2 tbsp chopped shallot
15 ml/1 tbsp dried shrimps, rinsed
115 g/4 oz minced pork
115 g/4 oz raw shelled prawns, chopped
30 ml/2 tbsp brown bean sauce
30 ml/2 tbsp rice wine vinegar
45 ml/3 tbsp fish sauce
75 g/3 oz palm sugar or soft dark
    brown sugar
30 ml/2 tbsp tamarind or
    lime juice
115 g/4 oz beansprouts

FOR THE GARNISH
2 spring onions, shredded
30 ml/2 tbsp fresh coriander leaves
2 heads pickled garlic (optional)
2-egg omelette, rolled and sliced
2 red chillies, seeded
    and chopped

1 Heat the oil in a wok. Break the vermicelli into small handfuls about 7.5 cm/3 in long. Deep fry in the hot oil until they puff up. Remove and drain on kitchen paper.

2 Leave 30 ml/2 tbsp of the oil in the wok, add the garlic, chillies, shallot and dried shrimps and fry until fragrant. Add the minced pork and stir-fry for 3–4 minutes until it is no longer pink. Add the chopped prawns and fry for 2 minutes. Remove the mixture from the wok and set aside.

3 To the same wok, add the brown bean sauce, rice wine vinegar, fish sauce and sugar. Bring to a gentle boil, stir to dissolve the sugar and continue to cook until syrupy.

4 Add the tamarind or lime juice to the wok and adjust the seasoning to taste. The sauce should be sweet, sour and salty. Reduce the heat.

5 Add the pork mixture and the beansprouts to the sauce in the wok and stir to coat well.

6 Add the rice vermicelli to the wok and toss gently to coat with the sauce without breaking the vermicelli too much.

7 Transfer the vermicelli to a warmed serving platter and garnish with shredded spring onions, coriander, pickled garlic (if liked), omelette strips and red chillies. Serve immediately.

Seafood Salad with Herbs

A fragrant and nourishing dish.

Serves 4–6

INGREDIENTS
250 ml/8 fl oz/1 cup fish stock or water
350 g/12 oz squid, cleaned and cut into rings
12 raw king prawns, shelled
12 scallops
50 g/2 oz bean thread noodles, soaked in
    warm water for 30 minutes
½ cucumber, cut into thin sticks
1 lemon grass stalk, finely chopped
2 kaffir lime leaves, finely shredded
2 shallots, finely sliced
juice of 1–2 limes
30 ml/2 tbsp fish sauce
30 ml/2 tbsp chopped spring onion
30 ml/2 tbsp fresh coriander leaves
12–15 fresh mint leaves, roughly torn
4 red chillies, sliced
fresh coriander sprigs, to garnish

1 Pour the stock or water into a medium-size saucepan, set over a high heat and bring to the boil. Cook each type of seafood separately for a few minutes. Drain and set aside.

2 Drain the noodles and cut into pieces about 5 cm/2 in long. Combine with the cooked seafood.

3 Add all the remaining ingredients, mix together well and serve garnished with the coriander sprigs.

Pomelo Salad

A pomelo resembles a grapefruit.

Serves 4–6

INGREDIENTS
30 ml/2 tbsp vegetable oil
4 shallots, finely sliced
2 garlic cloves, finely sliced
1 large pomelo
115 g/4 oz cooked shelled prawns
115 g/4 oz cooked crab meat
15 ml/1 tbsp roasted peanuts, ground
10–12 small fresh mint leaves
2 spring onions, finely sliced
2 red chillies, seeded and finely sliced
fresh coriander leaves
shredded fresh coconut (optional)

FOR THE DRESSING
30 ml/2 tbsp fish sauce
15 ml/1 tbsp palm sugar or soft
    dark brown sugar
30 ml/2 tbsp lime juice

1 Whisk together the dressing ingredients and set aside. Fry the shallots and garlic in the oil until golden and set aside.

2 Combine small pieces of pomelo with prawns, crab, peanuts, mint and shallot mixture. Dress the salad and sprinkle over the remaining ingredients.

Right: Seafood Salad with Herbs (top); Pomelo Salad

Tapioca Pudding

Lychees or the smaller, similar-tasting logans go well with this.

Serves 4

INGREDIENTS
115 g/4 oz/⅔ cup tapioca
475 ml/16 fl oz/2 cups water
175 g/6 oz sugar
250 ml/8 fl oz/1 cup coconut milk
pinch of salt
finely shredded rind of 1 lime, to decorate
250 g/9 oz prepared tropical fruits,
    to serve

1 Soak the tapioca in warm water for about 1 hour to swell. Drain thoroughly. Bring the water to the boil in a saucepan. Stir in the sugar and salt. Add the tapioca and coconut milk and simmer for 10 minutes or until the tapioca turns transparent.

2 Serve warm accompanied by tropical fruits and decorated with fine shreds of lime rind.

Fried Bananas

These delicious treats are sold at roadside stalls in Thailand.

Serves 4

INGREDIENTS
115 g/4 oz/1 cup plain flour
2.5 ml/½ tsp bicarbonate of soda
30 ml/2 tbsp sugar
1 egg
90 ml/6 tbsp water
30 ml/2 tbsp shredded coconut or
    15 ml/1 tbsp sesame seeds
4 firm bananas, peeled
oil, for frying
pinch of salt
fresh mint sprigs and fresh lychees,
    to decorate
30 ml/2 tbsp honey, to serve (optional)

1 Sift the flour, bicarbonate of soda and salt into a bowl. Stir in the sugar. Whisk in the egg and enough water to make a thin batter. Whisk in the coconut or sesame seeds.

2 Cut each banana in half lengthways and crossways. Dip in the batter, then fry in hot oil until golden brown.

3 Remove from the oil and drain on kitchen paper. Decorate with mint and lychees and serve with honey, if using.

Right: Tapioca Pudding (top);
Fried Bananas

Coconut Custard

This traditional dish can be baked or steamed and is often served with
sweet sticky rice and a selection of fruit such as mango and tamarillo.

Serves 4–6

INGREDIENTS
4 eggs
75 g/3 oz soft light brown sugar
250 ml/8 fl oz/1 cup coconut milk
5 ml/1 tsp vanilla, rose or
    jasmine extract
fresh mint leaves and icing sugar,
    to decorate
prepared tropical fruits,
    to serve

2 Strain the mixture and pour into
individual ramekins. Stand the
ramekins in a roasting tin. Pour hot
water into the tin to reach halfway up
the outsides of the ramekins.

1 Preheat the oven to 150°C/300°F/
Gas 2. Whisk the eggs and sugar in a
bowl until smooth. Add the coconut
milk and vanilla, rose or jasmine
extract and continue to whisk to
ensure that they are well blended.

VARIATION: If tropical fruits are
not in season you could substitute
strawberries, pears or peaches.

3 Bake for about 35–40 minutes or
until the custards are set. Test with a
fine skewer or cocktail stick. Remove
from the oven and leave to cool.

4 Turn out on to a plate, and
surround with fruit. Decorate with
mint leaves and icing sugar and serve.

Baked Rice Pudding

Black sticky rice gives this baked pudding a distinct character and an unusual nutty flavour.

Serves 4–6

INGREDIENTS
175 g/6 oz/¾ cup white or black
 sticky rice
30 ml/2 tbsp soft light
 brown sugar
250 ml/8 fl oz/1 cup water
475 ml/16 fl oz/2 cups coconut milk
3 eggs
30 ml/2 tbsp sugar

1 Put the rice, sugar, water and half the coconut milk in a saucepan. Bring the mixture to the boil and simmer for 15–20 minutes or until the rice has absorbed most of the liquid, stirring occasionally. Preheat the oven to 150°C/300°F/Gas 2.

2 Transfer the rice into an ovenproof dish. Mix together the eggs, remaining coconut milk and sugar in a bowl. Strain and pour evenly over the par-boiled rice.

3 Place the dish in a roasting tin. Pour in enough boiling water to come halfway up the sides of the dish. Cover the dish with foil and bake for about 35 minutes–1 hour or until the custard is set. Serve warm or cold.

Mango with Sticky Rice

Mangoes, with their delicate fragrance, blend especially well with coconut sticky rice.

Serves 4

INGREDIENTS
115 g/4 oz sticky white rice, washed and
 soaked in water overnight
175 ml/6 fl oz/¾ cup thick coconut milk
45 ml/3 tbsp sugar
2 ripe mangoes, peeled, stoned and sliced
pinch of salt
strips of lime rind, to decorate

1 Drain the rice and spread in an even layer in a steamer lined with muslin. Cover and steam for about 20 minutes or until tender.

2 Meanwhile, reserve 45 ml/3 tbsp of the top of the coconut milk and combine the rest with the sugar and salt in a pan. Bring to the boil, stirring until the sugar dissolves, then pour into a bowl to cool a little.

3 Turn the rice into a bowl and pour over the coconut mixture. Stir, then leave for about 10–15 minutes. To serve, place the mangoes on top of the rice and drizzle over the reserved coconut milk. Decorate with lime rind.

*Right: Baked Rice Pudding (top);
Mango with Sticky Rice*

This edition published by Southwater

Southwater is an imprint of
Anness Publishing Limited
Hermes House
88-89 Blackfriars Road
London, SE1 8HA
tel. 020 7401 2077
fax 020 7633 9499

Distributed in the UK by
The Manning Partnership
251-253 London Road East
Batheaston
Bath BA1 7RL
tel. 01225 852 727
fax 01225 852 852

Distributed in the USA by
Anness Publishing Inc.
27 West 20th Street
Suite 504, New York
NY 10011
tel. 212 807 6739
fax 212 807 6813

Distributed in Australia by
Sandstone Publishing
Unit 1, 360 Norton Street
Leichhardt
New South Wales 2040
tel. 02 9560 7888
fax 02 9560 7488

Southwater is an imprint of Anness Publishing Limited

© 2000 Anness Publishing Limited

A CIP catalogue record for this book
is available from the British Library

Publisher: Joanna Lorenz
Editor: Valerie Ferguson
Series Designer: Bobbie Colgate Stone
Designer: Andrew Heath
Production Controller: Joanna King

Recipes contributed by: Kit Chan

Photography: Thomas Odulate.

1 3 5 7 9 10 8 6 4 2

Printed and bound in Singapore

Notes:
For all recipes, quantities are given in both
metric and imperial measures and, where
appropriate, measures are also given in
standard cups
and spoons.
Follow one set, but not a mixture, because
they are not interchangeable.

Standard spoon and cup measures are level.

1 tsp = 5 ml   1 tbsp = 15 ml

1 cup = 250 ml/8 fl oz

Australian standard tablespoons are 20 ml.
Australian readers should use 3 tsp in place
of 1 tbsp for measuring small quantities of
gelatine, cornflour, salt etc.

Medium eggs are used
unless otherwise stated.